Succeeding at SATS

NATIONAL CURRICULUM
ENGLISH

Your guide to the KS2 National Curriculum Tests

Susan Power

Collins*Children'sBooks*
Copyright © HarperCollins Publishers Ltd 1997

Note for Pupils

What do the Key Stage 2 National Tests mean to you?

The tests help you check your progress in **English**, **Science** and **Mathematics** through Key Stage 2. By assessing your strengths and weaknesses they enable you to set your targets for future progress in these subjects. Your teachers will send the results of your test to your secondary school to help them decide the best subject group for you.

When will you take these tests?

They take place in early May of each year.

What do the English National Tests consist of?

The tests are divided into 3 main parts:

Reading test
time 1 hour

This sets questions on a selection of reading passages, and tests how you respond to different types of writing, including stories, poems, news articles, advertisements, instructions and other factual information.

Writing test
time 1 hour

You will be asked to write on 1 out of 2 or 3 topics, which will be any of the following:
- **imaginative** (e.g. a story)
- **descriptive** (e.g. a diary or a catalogue)
- **informative** (e.g. a report, a letter or a magazine article).

Spelling and Handwriting test
time Spelling 10 mins
time Handwriting 5 mins

You will be asked to fill in the missing words in a passage read to you. Using the same passage you will be expected to provide a sample of your handwriting.

Top Tips

- If you are told to ring an answer, **don't** tick or cross it.
- Use your planning sheet for notes. **Don't** write your story on it.
- Tackle each quesiton. **No answer means no marks**.
- If you can't answer a question, leave it and come back to it at the end.
- **Manage your time** - split up the test into small parts and do each part on a different day. If you choose to do it in one sitting, have a lunchtime break between papers.
- **Pace yourself**. Look over the paper first, get your bearings and **don't** spend too long on any question.
- Leave enough time to **check** your answers at the end.
- With an adult use the boxes in the margin of the test papers to insert the marks you have awarded yourself. Write a total at the bottom of the page, and transfer the totals to page 48 and the inside back cover.
- **Don't panic**. If you practise in your weaker areas you'll be ready for the real test.

What is a level?

While at school you will progress through 8 levels in each subject. By the end of Key Stage 2 you should expect to be between levels 3 and 5. The results give the level you can expect to be placed in for each subject.

What does this book do for you?

- It shows the layout of the tests, and the types of questions you can expect.
- It shows you how to follow instructions precisely.
- It gives you practice in writing the test, and the confidence that comes with preparation.
- It shows you how to assess your own answers.

How to use this book

Get an adult to read through the instructions for each section with you, and set you writing.
They should help you to assess your answers and determine your approximate level.

Reading Test

Instructions for the Reading Test

In this test you have to answer questions about:

- a story *(Passage A)*
- a set of instructions *(Passage B)*
- a description *(Passage C)*.

You will find the story *(A)*, the set of instructions *(B)* and the description *(C)*, in the booklet in the centre of this book (pages 19-28).
Carefully detach the booklet and refer back to it whilst you are answering the questions. You can also jot notes around it, if you find that helpful.
You will be asked to answer the questions in the following different ways:

- **ringed answers**
  Erik the Viking travelled the seas in a:

  | steamer | galley | submarine | **(Viking Longship)** |

- **short answers**
  When a *question* is followed by a short line like this:

  _____

  your *answer* will be short. It will be just one or two words.

- **longer answers**
  When a *longer answer* is needed, you will know by the length of the *longer lines*:

  _____
  _____

- **answers in boxes**
  For these answers, you will need to put in more information. This information will probably be in full sentences.

You have 15 minutes in total to read the extracts *(A)(B)(C)*.
You then have 30 minutes to complete all the questions.

Reading Test — Story (Passage A)

The Reading Test

The questions in this section are about the story:
Erik and the Sea Dragon (A)
Put a **ring around** the answers which **complete** the sentences.

1

Erik and his men were about to set off on their journey. When they were ready, they:

a)	b)	c)	d)
packed everything into the ship	celebrated by eating and drinking	put up the sails	looked forward to the journey

2

The seas they were to sail were:

a)	b)	c)	d)
rough	deep	unknown	huge

3

Soon they came to some thick mist. But there was something strange about the way the mist looked, because:

a)	b)	c)	d)
they could not see to the left or to the right	they could not see in front or behind	they had been travelling three nights and days	it was a different colour from usual

Story (Passage A) — Reading Test

4

Erik asked his men if they had ever seen such a mist, but none of them had. Then it thundered. Thorkhild spoke to Erik who was his:

a) captain b) sailor c) neighbour d) uncle

5

Erik agreed with Thorkhild that the thunder was strange because:

a) it was very loud b) there was no lightning c) it was above their heads d) the boat shook

6

The most surprising thing though, was that:

a) thunder always dies away b) it follows lightning c) there was something strange about it d) the thunder grew louder all the time

7

Soon the men noticed the sun, which kept moving in the sky. It had a black spot in the middle. As soon as they saw a second sun, they all realised that it must be the eyes of The Great Dragon of the North Sea.
They rowed away as fast as they could, but:

a) the mist was smoke from the dragon's mouth b) the dragon was huge c) they were afraid of the dragon d) the ship was sucked into the dragon's mouth

Reading Test — Story (Passage A)

8

When Erik turned to Ragnar Forkbeard to ask him what they should do, he turned white and ran away. Not even Erik, his true friend, realised that:

a)	b)	c)	d)
he was really a coward	he had lost his courage and his tongue	he had a good idea for getting rid of the dragon	he was just tired

These questions are about <u>events</u> in the story.

9

Write down three ways in which Ragnar Forkbeard showed that he had not lost his:

1) courage _____

_____

2) voice _____

_____

3) wits _____

_____

Story (Passage A) — **Reading Test**

These questions are about the <u>characters</u> in the story

10

1) Why did the other Viking sailors think that Ragnar Forkbeard had lost his wits?

_____

_____

2) What do you think made Ragnar Forkbeard decide upon such an unusual plan?

_____

_____

11

Why do you think Sven the Strong decided that they had 'had it now'?

_____

_____

12

Write down three different things that should have told the sailors that they were coming close to the Dragon of the North Sea.

1) _____

2) _____

3) _____

Reading Test — **Story (Passage A)**

These are questions to make you think about <u>how</u> the story is written.

13

Find two words, or groups of words, which make the dragon seem big and frightening.

1) _____

2) _____

☐ 2

14

In describing the events which led to the meeting with the Dragon of the North Sea, the author starts many sentences with 'And..' and 'But..' (Pages 21 and 22). Why might the author have chosen to do this?

_____
_____

☐ 1

15

What evidence shows that Erik was in charge of the other men? List words, phrases or events below.

_____
_____
_____
_____
_____

☐ 4

16

Why do you think that at the end of the story the author suggests that no one dared to accuse Ragnar Forkbeard ever again of losing his courage, his voice or his wits?

_____
_____

☐ 2

total ☐

Story (Passage A) — Reading Test

These questions are to find out what <u>you</u> think about the story.

17

Do you think that Erik and his men usually quarrelled?
Write your answer in the box. Use what you know about the men from the story to work out your answer.

```
_____
_____
_____
```

18

Would you like to have been one of the Viking sailors on that journey? Explain why, or why not. Use some of the events in the story to help you think out the answer.

```
_____
_____
_____
```

19

Ragnar Forkbeard's plan was very simple. Why do you think it was able to succeed against all the strength of the dragon, when all the other sailors' efforts failed? Explain your answer in the box below.

```
_____
_____
_____
```

20

This story is one from a book of short stories about Erik the Viking. Say what you enjoyed or disliked about the story. Answer in the box below.

```
_____
_____
_____
_____
```

Reading Test — Following Instructions (Passage B)

The questions on this page are about the instructions on how to make a model:
Make your own Viking Longship (B)

1

Before the instructions for making a model of a Viking Longship there is a list of items needed. Why is this?

_____
_____
_____

2

Why do you think that most sentences in this section are very short?

_____
_____

3

How is this useful to the person making the model?

_____
_____

4

Why do you think there are two instructions in the same sentence in number 8?

_____
_____
_____

Description (Passage C) — Reading Test

The questions on this page are about the passage:
Viking Ships (C)

1

Look at pages 26 and 27 of your reading booklet. They tell us that the Vikings grew up able to row and sail all kinds of boats. Why was this?

_____

_____

2

The information about Viking ships shows three different parts of the ship which helped it travel the seas. List them below.

1) _____

2) _____

3) _____

3

Viking ships were very useful for sailing in all kinds of water. Can you explain why?

_____

_____

_____

_____

Reading Test — Description (Passage C)

4

Look at the two different sections of information. Why do you think that the information on Viking Longships is set out very differently from the instructions on making a model?

_____

_____

_____

_____

_____

5

Do you think that the instructions for making a Viking Longship are suitable for children to follow? Why do you or why don't you, think so?
Give your full answer in the box.

Levels 3-5 — **Writing Test**

Instructions for the Writing Test

In this test, there is a choice of things for you to write about.

You must select <u>one</u> only.

There are also some sheets on which to plan your ideas.

The adult who is with you will show you how to use one of them for writing down your ideas before you start.

You will have 15 minutes to think and write down your ideas before you begin. A planning sheet is provided for you to do this.

After that, you will have 45 minutes to write about the title you have chosen.

The Story Writing Test

1) **Meeting with a dragon**

The story about Erik the Viking tells us about the time Erik and his men met a dragon. Now you write a story about meeting a dragon one day.
You may find the picture helpful.

These questions may give you some ideas:
- Where did you meet the dragon?
- Was it friendly or frightening?
- What did it look like?
- What happened?

2) **Lucky escape**

They must think of a plan. Time was growing short. If they were to escape, it must be now.

Base your story on the sentences above.

These questions may help you:
- Who are the main characters?
- Why do they have to escape?
- Where do they want to go to?
- Is the story going to be exciting?

3) **Lost in the mist**

Call your story 'Lost in the mist'.

Perhaps these questions will give you some ideas:
- Who are the main characters?
- Where does the story take place?
- Is it frightening to be lost?
- Are they found? How?

Levels 3-5 | **Story Writing** | **Writing Test**

The Story Planning Sheet

Write the title you have chosen for your story here:

Think about:

◆ the characters – can you describe them?

◆ the events – can you make them interesting?

◆ how your story begins and ends.

This space is for your ideas. Don't worry about writing in sentences.
Do not use this page for writing your actual story.

_____
_____
_____
_____
_____
_____
_____
_____
_____
_____
_____
_____

total

Writing Test: Information Writing

The Information Writing Test

4) **Our World**

We have learned a great deal about people, such as the Vikings, who lived long ago. Much of what we have learned about them has been from things we have found or dug up. These things have provided us with information about their homes, their beliefs and about how they lived. Another useful source of information about them has been provided by writings they have left behind.

Your school is going to organise a competition. The idea is that all the people entering write an article for the school magazine, providing information about what a typical home is like in 1997.

The winning article will be sent up in one of the next space probes. If there are beings in space, a message from us will inform them about what life is like for us on Earth.

Can you send a clear message?

Write a magazine article about what a home of today is really like.

Your writing should not only give clear information, but should be as varied and interesting as you can make it.

Information Writing | Writing Test

The Information Writing Planning Sheet

Write here the title for your magazine article:

This space is for writing down ideas on your magazine article. Don't worry about writing in sentences.
Here are some guidelines to help you:

A home – what kind of building is it? What is it made of?

_____

_____

The people in it – what are they like?

_____

_____

Different kinds of room – how are they used?

_____

_____

What is in some of them – what makes them different? Can you describe them in an interesting way?

_____

_____

Special events in the home – e.g. birthdays, religious festivals, visits by friends. What are they like? What do people do at these times?

_____

total

Handwriting/Spelling Test

Instructions for the Spelling Test

On the following page you will find a passage about a dragon in which there are spaces for you to fill in missing words.

The adult who is helping you with this test will find the same story in the Answer section (page 46) and will read it to you while you follow it in your booklet.

You will find that they will also read out the words which should go in the gaps.

They will read it to you twice, first at a normal speaking pace and, on the second reading, slowly enough for you to have time to write the spellings on your sheet.

When you have finished, you will be given an opportunity to check carefully, the words that you have written.

You have 10 minutes for this test.

Instructions for the Handwriting Test

You will find a short paragraph on page 20 which continues the story of the dragon.

Copy it out in your best handwriting.

Remember to be as neat as you can, and join the letters if you can do so.

Handwriting/Spelling Test

The Spelling Test

The Dragon

On a distant mountain there was a dark, murky cave. In this cave there was a sad old dragon.

The dragon was sad because he was _____ alone. Every day he _____ his treasure, but that was not enough. On this _____ day, life to the dragon seemed more unbearably _____ than ever. It was winter; it had snowed. Nothing outside _____ . The world _____ and the cavern was plunged into deep _____ . _____ he caught a muffled sound. Footsteps approached. Was it an _____ ? A figure _____ . It was Sven the Viking, hunting for treasure. He _____ into the entrance, not noticing the dragon. Soon he was fascinated by the _____ objects before him. Right at the top of the hoard lay the finest_____ of all, but they were out of reach. He climbed up some way and then stretched out his arm to its _____ extent, but as he reached out, the _____ pile gave way. He was so surprised that he _____ not keep his balance and fell with it, _____ landing on the floor with a loud _____, a cascade of gold tumbling to his feet. By now, the dragon had seen enough, so he _____ loudly to warn of his presence. The terrified Sven was then dismayed to see the creature's massive length advancing towards him. Had he been hiding in the corner _____ to kill the Viking?

19

total

Handwriting/Spelling Test

The Handwriting Test

This short paragraph continues the story of the dragon. Copy it out in your best handwriting.

Remember to be as neat as you can, and join the letters if you can do so.

Sven was so afraid at seeing a dragon appear from nowhere that he could not move. As the dragon drew closer, the Viking expected to be blasted by its fiery breath. The creature's mouth was wide open ready. Instead, he heard a strange wheezing sound. The dragon was laughing.

PUPIL PAPER ENDS HERE

total

Note for Parents

Reading Test Answers

◆ Read the Reading Extracts first. Go through the answers to the test and assess them together with your child. Award a mark. Insert the mark in the box provided alongside the question.

◆ Content is the most important criterion in determining how to award a mark. It is not important if your child's wording is unlike that in the specimen answers provided here.

◆ The answers show the steps your child would, ideally, have gone through in order to arrive at the answer. The objective in providing these explanations is to give your child insight into how to think through the questions logically.

Writing Test Answers

◆ Three sample essays are provided. Each shows how the writer's achievements are judged and awarded a level in *one* of three broad categories:

◆ Purpose and Organisation (page 36)

◆ Grammar (page 38)

◆ Style (page 40).

◆ See how each essay is awarded a level in a category. Look at the boxed explanations of how the essay meets the criteria for that particular level.

◆ Compare these with your child's essay. See if his/hers has these elements, or more. Use the Evaluation Assessment Criteria (pages 42-44) to determine your child's level in that category.

◆ The *Quick Guide...* summarises why the essay is at a level. Now, having scrutinised the sample and having consulted the *Assessment Criteria* award your child's level.

◆ Do this for each of the three criteria to arrive at a total mark for your child's essay.

Spelling and Handwriting Test Answers

Instructions for administering the test and the answers, are provided on the detachable page, 45.

Remember that the more your child participates in the evaluation, the better they will understand what is expected of them.

Reading Test Answers — Story (Passage A)

Tips and reminders

◆ Did you **read** the instruction that said, '**Put a ring around** the answers that **complete** the sentences'? **Don't tick** the correct box, **or underline**. Follow the instruction.

◆ Did you underline the **specific things** that you were asked to do? It will help if you isolate 'clue-words'.

◆ You get a mark for every point made. So, if **three** marks are allocated to the question, you have to make three correct points to be awarded three marks. The mark is shown by a ✓ or a ◯.

Erik and the Sea Dragon   pages 3--9

1 Erik and his men were about to set off on their journey. When they were ready, they:
a) packed everything into the ship   b) **celebrated by eating and drinking** (ringed)   c) put up the sails   d) looked forward to the journey

When the men were ready, they dragged the boat back into the water and had a feast. Look for an answer that tells you this. You won't find the exact words, so look for a phrase that **means the same.** Packing everything into the ship is not the same as dragging it into the water, so a) is wrong. 'Celebrated by feasting and drinking,' means the same as 'had a feast', so b) is the answer.

2 The seas they were to sail were:
a) rough   b) deep   c) **unknown** (ringed)   d) huge

The passage says the boat 'sailed off into **uncharted** seas'. Check if 'uncharted' appears in a box. If not, look in the boxes for a word that **means the same.**

3 Soon they came to some thick mist. But there was something strange about the way the mist looked, because:
a) they could not see to the left or to the right   b) they could not see in front or behind   c) they had been travelling three nights and days   d) **it was a different colour from usual** (ringed)

Always look for '**clue-words**'. What is **strange** about the **thick mist? Eliminate** options that don't answer the question. Options a) and b) don't apply to a **strange** mist, so they aren't correct, and c) has nothing to do with the question. Option d) explains what is strange about the mist.

4 Erik asked his men if they had ever seen such a mist, but none of them had. Then it thundered. Thorkhild spoke to Erik who was his:
a) **captain** (ringed)   b) sailor   c) neighbour   d) uncle

You have to **deduce** what the correct answer is. Options c) and d) may be correct, **but** we have no information about this. Option b) is a possibility. The passage refers to 'Erik's men', but there is no similar reference to Thorkhild's men. Eric therefore is in charge of all the men including Thorkhild.

5 Erik agreed with Thorkhild that the thunder was strange because:
a) it was very loud   b) **there was no lightning** (ringed)   c) it was above their heads   d) the boat shook

Your answer must show why the thunder was **strange and** what **Eric** said about it. Options a) and c) are not strange. Thunder is usually loud and does sound above one's head. Go back to the question. It asks why **Eric** agrees that the thunder is strange. He says nothing about the shaking of the boat. But he **does** say that whilst thunder always follows lightning, in this case, **there was no lightning**.

Story (Passage A) — Reading Test Answers

6 The most surprising thing though, was that:

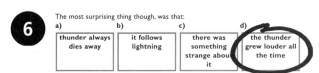

a) thunder always dies away
b) it follows lightning
c) there was something strange about it
d) **the thunder grew louder all the time** *(circled)*

Continue with the line of thought from the previous question. Identify not what is strange about the thunder, but what is **strangest** about the thunder. This is the 'clue-word'. Again, you are working with words/phrases that have similar meaning. 'Surprising' and 'strangest' have a similar meaning. You have to look for what Thorkhild says that means 'surprising'.

7 Soon, the men noticed the sun, which kept moving in the sky. It had a black spot in the middle. As soon as they saw a second sun, they all realised that it must be the eyes of The Great Dragon of the North Sea. They rowed away as fast as they could, but:

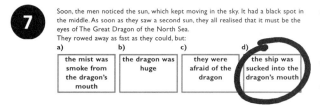

a) the mist was smoke from the dragon's mouth
b) the dragon was huge
c) they were afraid of the dragon
d) **the ship was sucked into the dragon's mouth** *(circled)*

Although we can safely **assume** that they were afraid, it does not actually **say** they were, so c) is not correct. It does seem as though all the other options could be right, but which one **is**? The question asks specifically what happened **after** they rowed away. Only one option fits: d).

8 When Erik turned to Ragnar Forkbeard to ask him what they should do, he turned white and ran away. Not even Erik, his true friend, realised that:

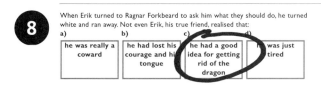

a) he was really a coward
b) he had lost his courage and his tongue
c) **he had a good idea for getting rid of the dragon** *(circled)*
d) he was just tired

You have to isolate **a key point** in the story. Not only did the men **not** realise that Ragnar had a good idea and had **not** lost his wits, **neither did Erik**. **If** you show that **you understand this point**, then **you understand a main point of the story.**

9 Write down three ways in which Ragnar Forkbeard showed that he had not lost his:

1) courage — He climbed to the top of the mast and faced the dragon ✓
2) voice — He shouted at the dragon ✓
3) wits — He thought he had a good plan by making the dragon sneeze ✓

Look at what Ragnar **actually did.** You are asked to give reasons that **show** that he had not lost his courage. You won't earn marks if you write what he **said**, i.e. 'I have neither lost my courage nor my tongue.' You must indicate what he **did**.

10
1) Why did the other Viking sailors think that Ragnar Forkbeard had lost his wits?
   He ran towards the dragon carrying pillows ✓

2) What do you think made Ragnar Forkbeard decide upon such an unusual plan?
   He knew that to use strength was useless ✓

Think about **what kind of people** the characters are and **what kind of things they do**, that are in keeping with their character.

11 Why do you think Sven the Strong decided that they had 'had it now'?

He felt they had had it, because there was no one strong enough to fight the dragon. ✓

OR They had made the dragon angry.
You need to understand the meaning of the expression, 'to have had it'. If you understand it **literally**, you will think it means that the men had physically taken possession of something. That expression doesn't make sense in this story. The writer uses the expression **colloquially** (in the way we usually use it) to mean, 'they had no chance left'.

Reading Test Answers — Story (Passage A)

12. Write down three different things that should have told the sailors that they were coming close to the Dragon of the North Sea.
  1) The mist was coloured ✓
  2) There was strange thunder without lightning ✓
  3) There were two suns in the sky. ✓

When pushed for time, it is tempting **to try and remember** what you had read in the passage. **It is better to check back** to the passage. Take the trouble, because it is fairly easy to gain these three marks..

13. Find two words, or groups of words, which make the dragon seem big and frightening.
  1) huge jaws ✓
  2) suns for eyes ✓

(Any two of the following)
huge jaws; suns for eyes; fiery jaws; roars of thunder; great fiery throat; loomed over the ship
A **quick skim-read** of the passage will be enough to help you find the answers you need here.

14. In describing the events which led to the meeting with the Dragon of the North Sea, the author starts many sentences with 'And.' and 'But.' (Pages 21 and 22). Why might the author have chosen to do this?
Every sentence adds more information, until the clues add up to solve the mystery that it's a dragon. ✓

OR Words like, 'And' and 'But', hold the reader's interest, suggesting that the author hasn't quite finished what he wants to say and is building up to something.
OR The mystery is solved by the appearance of the dragon and by how it is finally overcome, but before this, the author keeps the reader guessing.
You should make one of the three points above, in your own words. You might want to think hard about this question. If you are not sure what to write and want more time to think about the answer, leave it, and come back to it later.

15. What evidence shows that Erik was in charge of the other men? List words, phrases or events below.
  When it suggests Erik is in charge, e.g. 'Erik's men.' ✓
  When Erik seems to take the lead. The men obey him, e.g. 'To the oars,' said Erik. ✓
  When the men go to him for information, or to raise a point, e.g. 'Thorkhild came to Erik and said... .' ✓
  When Erik takes a decsion for the others, e.g. 'Erik saw it was no good. He... .' ✓

The answers aren't always obvious. You need to **interpret what the author says**, as meaning that Erik is in charge Sift through the information to find examples of Erik's leadership. You don't have to give reasons for your answer, or back your opinion with evidence. You simply have to **list them.**

16. Why do you think that at the end of the story the author suggests that no one dare accuse Ragnar Forkbeard ever again of losing his courage, his voice or his wits?
  They knew that he was brave. ✓
  He had done something they could not do. ✓

OR
He had killed the dragon.
They had come to respect him.
Show that you understand **how** the author reveals, step by step, that Ragnar was not a coward.
Even though you are asked what **you** think, you still have to give a viewpoint that can be backed up from the facts in the story.

Story (Passage A) — Reading Test Answers

17. Do you think that Erik and his men usually quarrelled? Write your answer in the box. Use what you know about the men from the story to work out your answer.

No, they did not usually quarrel.	✓
They consulted one another about their problems.	✓
They needed to work together to save themselves.	✓

Look at the **sort of things** they **usually did together** and then use them as examples. You are given several possible examples above that you could have used in your examples. You could ask yourself, 'Would they have got things done, if they had been arguing all the time?'

18. Would you like to have been one of the Viking sailors on that journey? Explain why, or why not. Use some of the events in the story to help you think out the answer.

Yes, I would have liked to have been a Viking,	✓
because I could have had many exciting adventures,	✓
and travelled to unknown places.	✓

OR

No, I would not have liked to have been a Viking, ✓
because there would have been frightening experiences, dangers, ✓
and it would have been uncomfortable. ✓

Think about the story, **and then give your opinion**. It also tests how well you entered into **the spirit of the story.**

The answer to this question can be 'yes' or 'no'. In order to gain a mark though, you must **back up** your answer **with evidence** from the story that you understood something of what a Viking's life was like. Above are some examples of the kind of things you might have said as evidence.

19. Ragnar Forkbeard's plan was very simple. Why do you think it was able to succeed against all the strength of the dragon, when all the other sailors' efforts failed? Explain your answer in the box below.

It succeeded because the others tried to use their strength.	✓
He looked for a weakness in the dragon.	✓
He used his brains, not his strength to overcome it.	✓

First, decide **what was his great plan.** Say how it was different from what the others did.
Finally, work out that it was not the usual way a Viking would have fought. They were accustomed to using their strength and that would not have worked against the dragon. If your answer is slightly different from this, but makes sense, you can still get your marks. This is where an adult can help you decide.

20. This story is one from a book of short stories about Erik the Viking. Say what you enjoyed or disliked about the story. Answer in the box below.

Yes, I liked the story.	✓
It was exciting. There was suspense when we did not know what was in the mist.	✓
It was quite funny when the others thought Ragnar Forkbeard had gone mad.	✓

OR

No, I didn't like it. ✓
I do not like stories about people who lived a long time ago. ✓
Modern stories with space ships and machines are much more exciting. ✓

There can be different answers to this question. Those given above are suggested answers. Both can be right as well! Whichever you choose, you **must say why. Back up your opinion** with **examples** from the events and characters in the story. You need to state your opinion, yes or no.

Instructions (Passage B)

Make your own Viking Longship   page 10

1. Before the instructions for making a model of a Viking Longship there is a list of items needed. Why is this?

A list is given so you can be organised. It is better to know in advance what you need so you can collect everything first. The model will be easier to make if you are prepared.

Use your **common sense** to answer this question as you **won't** find the answer in the instructions.
Think out your **own** answer. There are several different correct answers. Your answer should be the same as, or similar to, those given here. Ask the adult who is helping you to decide with you if **your** answer shows sufficient common sense to earn a mark.

2. Why do you think that most sentences in this section are very short?

Most of the sentences are very short because each has a single instruction. You do one thing at a time. It helps you to understand what to do.

Put yourself in the position of the person making the ship. Ask yourself, 'Would **I** prefer to have short sentences given me in these instructions? If so, why?'

3. How is this useful to the person making the model?

By giving only one instruction at a time it makes it easier for a person to follow all the instructions.

Think about what the person making the ship has to do, to carry out the instruction. Ask yourself, 'If these were two separate instructions instead of one, would I be able to do the activity as easily?'

4. Why do you think there are two instructions in the same sentence in number 7?

There are two instructions because you need to do two things at the same time.

Look at the picture often. It will help with your answer. Don't forget, diagrams **are part of** the instructions!

Description (Passage C)

Viking Ships   pages 11-12

1 Look at pages 26 and 27 of your reading booklet. They tell us that the Vikings grew up able to row and sail all kinds of boats. Why was this?

The Vikings grew up able to row and sail all kinds of boats because they lived near water, rivers, lakes and the sea.

The **clue-word** that gets you one mark for this answer is 'lived'. It is not enough to know that they had been familiar with the sea all their lives, you need to say that it was because they **lived close to** the sea. The only reason they were familiar with the sea is **because** they lived close to it.

2 The information about Viking ships shows three different parts of the ship which helped it travel the seas. List them below.

1) *the sail*
2) *the rudder*
3) *the oar*

Look at **all** the information to find these answers. Pictures give information **too**! That's a tip to help you find all the information you need to answer this question.

3 Viking ships were very useful for sailing in all kinds of water. Can you explain why.

Viking ships were useful for sailing in all kinds of water because they had a deep draught so they could sail into shallow water or, they were designed not to need deep water. The bottom of the boat was very flat.

This answer has two different facts taken from different parts of the information. You won't always find the answer in the same place.

4 Look at the two different sections of information. Why do you think that the information on Viking Longships is set out very differently from the instructions making a model?

The information is set out differently because to make the model, you need to follow all the instructions in the right order or, the pictures are numbered so that you can follow the instructions for making a Viking ship. You don't have to follow in any special order the information on the Viking longship.

Look back at **both** sections of information **as instructed in the question**. First, think about **ways** in which they are different, then think about the **reasons** for this.

5 Do you think that the instructions for making a Viking Longship are suitable for children to follow? Why do you or why don't you, think so? Give your full answer in the box.

The pictures are clear; each stage is numbered; the language is easy to follow; one instruction is given at a time.

Look back at both the **pictures and** the **writing.** Think about doing the model **yourself**. Would you be able to do it from the instructions?
How does this way of presenting instructions make them easy to understand? That is what children would be expecting from them.

Writing Test Answers — Imaginative Writing — Level 3

Notice the clear beginning to the story:
* 'One day I was on the way to school.'
The writer tells the reader what she was doing when she met the dragon, and why she was there.

At Level 3: **There should be a clear beginning.**

The writer describes the dragon. She gives details of **his appearance**. He is:
* 'purple with green spots' and has 'blue eyes'.
The writer is **aware of the dragon's feelings:**
* 'It was crying.'
The dragon also **has a reason** (a motive) for being there. It is lonely.

At Level 3: **The characters should show some detail.**

See how this story uses speech marks correctly. This is a requirement **for level 4**. You need to meet all the requirements for level 3 and more than one requirement for level 4 to be placed in that category though. Look at the Assessment Criteria Charts on pp 43 to see what you would have had to include in your essay for a 4-rating.

At Level 3: **Inverted commas may or may not be correctly used.**

Don't just tell things. Add descriptive detail to bring the story to life.
* 'I went through the **side** gate.'
* 'The dragon had **purple** wings.'
* '**Suddenly,** I saw... .'
The highlighted words are all details that **make the story interesting.**
How does your story compare? Go through and pick out all those words that **make your story real.**

At Level 3: **Some descriptive detail should be evident.**

Dragon in the playground

One day I was on the way to School with my mum and my dad. I got to the school and I was early, but my mum and my dad where late for work. So they had to leave me at the school on my oney at the school. I went through the side gate to made my way through the plants to the playground. I had a great surprise, there was a dragon layin a-sleep on the playground. Well it was a little bit of a surprise because it was frightening as well because noone except me was there. I went over to the dragon, it was purple, with green spots, it had blue eyes and sharp white teeth, with purple wings. Then suddenly I saw that he was getting up, I would of liked to run away but it was crying. I went over to it and it talked to me. It said "Hello my name is smaug and would you like to come and play with me."
I said "I can not play with you but you can be my friend for ever if you like, I have got to work at school now." I was going away when the dragon began to cry again. I saw my friend coming round the side gate I left it open. She ran away when she saw the dragon and I shouted to

---

Quick guide to test this story for **Purpose and Organisation**

Note to the parent

Looking at this story for a Level 3 rating
* The writing is relevant to the topic.
* There is a clear beginning.
* There is a simple ending.
* Some details of the setting are present.
* Some details of the characters are included e.g. a physical description, and feelings.

All the elements for level 3 Purpose and Organisation are present.

Looking at this story for a Level 4 rating
* A beginning, middle and ending are all shown. Events **are** logical.
* Paragraphs are **not** used.
* Characters are **not** clearly detailed or developed.

Elements of level 4 are present, but not enough to warrant a level 4 rating. All elements must be present.

This story scored: 12/18

Your child's story scored: /18

Imaginative Writing — Writing Test Answers

Look at **punctuation** in this story. **Just over half** the full stops are **used correctly**. More than half your story needs to show correct use of:
* **capital letters**
* **full stops** and,
* **question marks.**

At Level 3: **At least half the sentences should be correctly punctuated**.

See how the story of the dragon **is connected to** the story title and to the instructions on page 14. The writer was told to write about:
* where she found it
* whether it was friendly or frightening
* what it looked like and,
* what happened.

Now look at your story. Did you follow those instructions?

At Level 3: **Writing should be relevant to the title**.

---

her many of times but she cept on running and running, till she got to a phone box and ringed up the people who catchs dragons and puts them in dragon Jail. The men came along I head them coming round because I heard the van coming. I tried to hide it everywhere but it was to big. The men came along and they said to me "do not be afraid I have come for the dragon to take it to dragon Jail it will be warm in dragon Jail."
The dragon thought they where going to kill it so it tried to fly away but he could not fly, I wass frightened that smaug was going to be killled. The men could not handle the dragon so they had to get a dager out of the van and kill it. I was very frightened I didn't want smaug to die he was my best friend but they killed it and there was blood coming out of it but the blood was purple they berred the dragon that day and I was heart broken that I had lost my friend but I thought it was my best friend. My mum came and picked me up She keeped me home for two days, I take flowers to the dragon every day now.

Include more than just one idea in some of the sentences. **Connect different ideas** together. Examples of how the writer has done this in the story are:
* 'I heard them coming round, **because** I heard the van coming,' instead of:
  'I heard them coming round. I heard the van coming.'
* 'I was going away **when** the dragon began to cry,' instead of:
  'I was going away. The dragon began to cry.'

At Level 3: **Some sentences should express more than a simple structure of one idea.**

Look at **the way sentences** in the story **begin**. Can you see how many of them start with 'I'? For example:
* 'I got to the school and I was early..... .'
* 'I went through the side gate..... .'

Of course you can start a sentence with 'I', but too many sentences like that can be monotonous. Try varying the way in which you start sentences.
* 'It was early when I got to school, so I... .'
* 'The side gate was open so I went through... .'

At Level 3: **Some sentences should have a varied structure.**

Here is an example of **how to put the story in a setting** that works well:
'I had to make my way **through the plants** to the playground.'
Did you think about **where** the events in **your story** were happening?
Make sure your reader is as clear as you are, about where in the story events are taking place.

At Level 3: **Some detail of the setting should be provided**

Look at the **simple ending**:
* 'I take flowers to the dragon every day now.'
A single sentence tells the reader that the story is finished.
Always **make sure that your story ends properly**.

At Level 3: **A simple ending must be included.**

Writing Test Answers — Informative Writing — Level 4

Look **at the beginning** of this story. The reader knows **exactly** what the writer is describing. The introduction gives detail about the outside of the house: where it is and how old it is. In a descriptive essay, the beginning of the story should take you straight in to the story. **Get to the point** of what the description is about.

At Level 4: **There should be a proper beginning, middle and end to the story.**

Use some good descriptive words as this writer has done:
* 'very large, silver birch',
* 'beautiful colours'; 'blue umbrella'; 'solid, pine door'. Now look at your story.
Pick out examples of **good descriptive words** that make your writing more lively.

At Level 4: **Descriptions should be more complex than in levels 3. Words should evoke feelings, sensations and impressions.**

Be aware that you need to **express yourself differently** when writing and when speaking. Look at the way ideas are expressed in this story. 'We have a very long garden,' instead of, 'We've got a long garden.' The writer **uses the language of writing and not the spoken language** of for example, the playground.

At Level 4: **Awareness of the difference between the written and the spoken language should be shown.**

Use commas accurately to separate items on a list:
* 'There are rooms downstairs: the lounge, the dining-room and kitchen.'
If you include a list, make sure each item is separated by a comma, except for the last two where you use 'and' instead. N.B. Don't put lots of lists in your writing, they can be boring. YAWN!

At Level 4: **Commas should be used correctly to separate items on a list.**

My House

My house was built in 1936 by a local builder it is a three bedroom semi-detached. We have a very long garden with a garage at the end and also a very large silver birch tree that is bluey-green colour. We have a patio which is a paved area with flower beds that have beautiful colours pink, red, yellow etc around the edges of patio, in the summer we sit around a table and eat our lunch under a blue blue umbrella which keeps the sun of us.
To enter the house we go through a solid pine door which leads into the hall. On a shelf is the telephone which is used to phone up our friends to talk to them we pick up the hand set push the number buttons it will ring. If my friend is home they will pick up the phone and speck. There are three rooms down stairs the louge, dinning room and kitchen. In the dining room there is a big room table with six chairs around it for me and my family to sit around and eat breakfast, lunch or tea. At christmas time when nan, Grandad, Anuties and Uncles come for

---

Quick guide to test this story for **Grammar**

Note to the parent

Looking at this story for a Level 4 rating
Punctuation:
* **Commas** have been correctly **used in** writing **lists** of items.
* **Three quarters of the sentences are correctly punctuated.**
* The author has **used the correct** narrative **voice** throughout. Either: 'I' or 'We' or 'He' or, 'She'.

All the elements for level 4 Grammar are present.

Looking at this story for a Level 5 rating
* **Full stops** are **not used correctly enough** in all but two sentences on the first page.
* **Commas should have been used** to divide sentences, 'To enter the house , we go through.....'

Some of the elements for level 5 are here. Check the Assessemt Criteria for Grammar level 5 on page 44, to find what is missing.

This story scored:

5 / 6

Your child's story scored:

6

Informative Writing — Writing Test Answers

Join sentences containing **similar ideas together** to form one sentence.
Totally separate ideas must be written as separate sentences though. Look at this example:
'We have a patio which is a paved area with flower beds that have beautiful colours pink, red yellow etc around the edgesof the patio, in the summer we sit around the table... .'
Here, the writer has joined **two totally separate ideas** together **in one sentence!**

> **At Level 4:** *Most sentences should use full stops and capital letters correctly*.

Notice how the writer **puts ideas into paragraphs**. A paragraph is a group of sentences all about the same idea.
The Planning sheet actually helps you divide your ideas into sections, but the writer has used another way:
* outside
* downstairs
* upstairs.

> **At Level 4:** *Events and ideas should be organised logically*

diner we extend the table so we can get ten chairs around. Also we have a christmas tree in the window.

Go up the stairs onto the landing and you will see four doors. The first room is the bathroom where I wash myself and clearn my teeth in there bath, toilet and hand basin also we keep shower gel, shampoo, soap and tooth paste. The next bedroom is my sisters Kylie. She has one of the big rooms to keep all her toys in. She is 9 years old and go's to Junior School. My Mum's and Dad's room has the biggest bedroom with a double bed in a wardrobe and a table with a lamp. My bedroom is the smallest room in the house it is very compact. I have a built in wardrobe, three shelfs for my books, three conner shelfs and a desk and chair where I do my homework at an evening. Also we have a flat the top of are house to keep things in. This is my house which is similar to many other houses in 1997.

Take a closer look at the **sentences** in the story. Many **begin differently**:
'My.....', 'We,,,', 'To,,,,.' 'On.....'
Aim to do this too. Don't contrive to make every sentence different, but do **introduce variety**. Your writing will be interesting to read.

> **At Level 4:** *Writing should make use of interesting and varied forms.*

Sentence structure is important at level 4. Some are longer than others. Some are joined together. The shape of the sentences changes.

> **At Level 4:** *Writing should make use of interesting and varied forms.*

This writer uses the present tense consistently. She does not change from past to present or vice versa.

> **At Level 4:** *Correct use of tenses is required.*

Round the writing off at the end. It should feel **finished.**
This is called a conclusion. Did you do this? A good way is to refer back to the title.

> **At Level 4:** *The story, not only has a clear ending, but a clear beginning and middle as well.*

Writing Test Answers — Imaginative Writing — Level 5

Go straight into the story as this writer does. In the first paragraph he **includes important details** which the reader needs **to make sense of the story**. He:
* is visiting Scotland from Liverpool (the setting)
* has been suffering from asthma (the background)
* is staying with his grandmother (more background)
* is out in the country walking, and finds an entrance in the rocks (introducing the main theme).

The beginning is interesting because he starts with **a conversation** - between himself and his gran.

*At Level 5: **The introduction should be clear and may experiment**, e.g. by using **conversation, action and description**.*

Notice the **variety and interest** in the different elements of the story. It contains **conversation, action, description.** All the points of **the plot** follow after each other in **a logical pattern**.

*At Level 5: **The middle (body) of the story should be logical and varied**.*

Commas are used to **separate sentences**. This is necessary when a more complex sentence pattern is used:
* 'There, half submerged in a pool of water, was an enormously large.. .'

*At Level 5: **Commas should be used correctly, to divide sentences**.*

Can you **use vocabulary imaginatively,** as this writer has done?
* 'I strolled happily down dusty, old lanes.'
* 'tongues of flame spurted....'
* 'a frenzy of fear.'
* 'edged towards the stairs.'

Notice these examples, but there are others that **bring the story to life** and make it flow well.

*At Level 5: **Vocabulary should be varied and chosen with effect**.*

The Last Scottish Dragon

"May I go out today?" I said.
"Well alright," my gran said in her soft Scottish accent. What a change from Liverpool, I thought, as I strolled happily down dusty old lanes through the hills. I was in Scotland for a change of air because of me suffering from Asma. I was staying with my gran in her little white-washed cottage. I came round a bend in the lane and saw an entrance in the rocks.

   Cautiously I stooped down and went through the entrance in the rocks. It led down a flight of steps, that were covered in slimy old weeds. It got colder and damper as I went further down. At the end of the flight of steps it was pitch dark and I could not see a thing. I struck a match and looked around.

   "What ye doing here?" said a voice. I wheeled round and looked to see where the voice had come from. There, half submerged in a pool of water, was an enormously big, dark green, scaly dragon. little toungs of flame spurted from its nose, each time it breathed, I turned and ran towards the stairs in a frenzy of fear.

Quick guide to test this story for Style

Looking at this story for a Level 5 rating
* **Sentences** are **varied**.
* **Vocabulary** is **varied** and used for effect.
* The writer **has made use of** both **standard and local English** for effect.

All the style elements required for level 5 are displayed.

Looking at this story for a Level 6 rating
* There is **some use of metaphor** e.g. 'tongues of flame'.
* The choice of verbs is **particularly varied, to give subtle shades of meaning**.
* The sentence structure is varied, but not sufficiently to show **very subtle effects**.
* Dialect is used, but does not show evidence of **absolute familiarity with dialect**.

Some elements of level 6 are present.

This story scored: 6 / 6

Your child's story scored: 6

Note to the parent

Imaginative Writing — Writing Test Answers

Look at the wording of these two conversations. It shows that the writer understands the difference between **standard English and dialect**:
- 'There's nowt to be afraid of.. .' (dialect)
- Sorry...I will go,' I said. (standard English).

He **uses this** effectively **to introduce variety** and **to draw** convincing **word-portraits** of the characters.

> **At Level 5:** *The writer should show an ability to choose between standard English and dialect.*

"There's nowt to be afraid of young man, I do not bite," the dragon said.

"Sorry for coming, I will go," I said in a whimpering sort of voice as I edged towards the stairs.

"And what's the rush, stay and talk to me, I could do with the company," the dragon said.

"Okay," I said as I realised the dragon was not fierce and would not kill me. I stayed talking to the dragon for some time. In this time I learned that his name was Rob McRob and was the last dragon left in Scotland. Then saying I had to go for my tea, I left and ran up the steps and all the way home, knowing I was late.

"How come your so late? I've been worried," gran said as I ran through the door. "If you have found something so wonderful that you stayed away four hours it's a shame seeing that you leave at six o'clock tomorrow morning."

I never saw the dragon again, but in dreams I often visit him and fly on his back over the mountains of Scotland. The End.

Did you write a conclusion to end your story? At level 5, it should be **connected to the main story line.** In this example, revisiting Scotland and the dragon in dreams, is a good way of **rounding off the writing.** The story should never end abruptly, or tail off into nothingness....... !

> **At Level 5:** *The conclusion should be clear.*

Note how the **punctuation** in this story is almost **absolutely correct**. Only one capital letter has been forgotten.

> **At Level 5:** *There should be very few lapses of punctuation and capital letters.*

Quite clearly, the writer **knows how to use paragraphs**. Each 'set of happenings' is separated into a paragraph:
- He sets the scene for the story.
- He explores the cave.
- He encounters the dragon.
- He and the dragon chat to one another. Notice how the speech sentences have separate paragraphs.
- He leaves the dragon and returns home.
- He is reunited with his gran. Notice that he explains nothing to her.
- The adventure never truly ends. He meets the dragon again and travels with him in his dreams.

Now look at your essay. Are the **main ideas and events** sorted into **separate** paragraphs?

> **At Level 5:** *Paragraphs should be used correctly to separate the main ideas of the plot.*

Look at the opening words of the paragraph starting:
- "Okay," I said.

It is **set out** correctly, **with speech marks and** with the separating comma. Remember that when you are writing, you use double speech marks " ". In printed books, single marks are used.

> **At Level 5:** *Speech marks and the separating comma should be used.*

Have you noticed **the shape of the sentences?** They are very varied:
- 'I stayed talking to the dragon for some time.'
- 'Then saying I had to go for tea, I left and ran up the steps and all the way home, knowing I was late.'

Several ideas are contained in the second sentence, but the writer doesn't write 'and' all the time.

> **At Level 5:** *Sentences should be varied.*

Writing Assessment Criteria

Note to the Parent
Use the criteria listed on the following three pages to assess the level of your child's writing. Determine which level best fits the story in each of the categories: Purpose, Grammar or Style.
Remember, the writing has to fulfil all the criteria of that level, to be awarded the marks allocated to it.

Level 3

Imaginative and Descriptive Writing

1. Purpose and Organisation Maximum Marks 12
As a whole the writing shows evidence of:
* a clear beginning.
* a simple ending.
* some details of the setting.
* some details of the characters such as: physical appearance, feelings and motives.

2. Grammar Maximum Marks 4
* At least half the sentences show that the child knows how to use full stops and capital letters.
* The child writer **may** be using inverted commas, but not necessarily correctly.

3. Style Maximum Marks 4
* Sentences are moving away from the very simple structure of a single idea.
* Sentences are joined by words such as: 'but', 'when', 'because'.
* Some descriptive detail is evident, e.g.
  'a cold morning',
  'he walked quickly.. '.

Informative Writing

Note to the Parent
No question on writing a letter has been set in this paper. This could be an option in the actual test. The criteria for assessing Informative Writing and Letters differ from Imaginative and Descriptive Writing in the Purpose and Organisation category only. They are listed here and on the following two pages.

1. Purpose and Organisation Maximum Marks, 12
* There is an introduction.
* Points are logically organised.
* In a letter, some understanding of the format is shown.

Writing Assessment Criteria

Level 4

Imaginative and Descriptive Writing

1. Purpose and Organisation   Maximum Marks, 15
* There is some use of paragraphs to separate the beginning and ending of the story from the rest.
* Events should be organised logically.
* The story should show a beginning, middle and an end.
* The actions of the characters affect each other.
* Characters are clearly described by what they say, what others say of them, or by added comments of the child writer.

2. Grammar   Maximum Marks, 5
* Use of tense is consistent. It does not change from past to present, or vice versa.
* Use of pronouns is correct - either 'I' or, 'he/she' throughout the story.
* Most of the sentences use full stops, capital letters and question marks correctly.
* Commas are used correctly to separate items on a list.
* If speech is used, speech marks are used correctly at the beginning and end of words spoken, **most** of the time.

3. Style   Maximum Marks, 5
* Greater awareness of written, as opposed to spoken language is shown, e.g.
  'John's got a new bike' - **spoken**:
  John received a new bicycle for his birthday - **written**.
* Joining words are used to emphasise or to order, e.g.
  If he were to do that, something else would happen.
  When he had finished, he went on to.. .
* More detailed and effective use of vocabulary adds quality to the story, e.g.
  At the end of a **rough** path stood a **beautiful, old** cottage.

Informative Writing

1. Purpose and Organisation   Maximum Marks, 15
* There is an introduction and a conclusion.
* Points made and facts given are related to one another.
* A fairly secure understanding of the letter format is shown.
* Some paragraphing is used.

Writing Assessment Criteria

Level 5

Imaginative and Descriptive Writing

1. Purpose and Organisation   Maximum Marks, 18
- Paragraphs are used correctly, to separate the main ideas of the plot.
- Events may be more complicated, e.g.
  'a flashback in time'.
- The introduction is clear and may experiment, e.g. using conversation or events which only become clear later in the story.
- The middle is logical and varied, containing conversation, action and description.
- The conclusion should be clear.

2. Grammar   Maximum Marks, 6
- There are very few lapses in use of punctuation and capital letters.
- Commas are used to divide sentences, e.g.
  On receiving the letter, she was overjoyed.
- Speech marks are used correctly.
- The separating comma is also used, e.g.
  "I've got a new puppy," said John.
  John said, "I've got a new puppy."

Style   Maximum Marks, 6
- Sentences are varied, e.g.
  'He caught sight of the mysterious figure..... '.
  'As he caught sight of the mysterious figure.....'.
  'On catching sight of the mysterious figure....'.
- Vocabulary is varied and carefully chosen for effect.
- The writer shows the ability to choose between standard English for telling the story, and the use of speech and dialect for effect.

Informative Writing

1. Purpose and Organisation   Maximum Marks, 15
- Work shows a clear understanding of explanatory writing.
- Main points are developed in detail and linked e.g.
  'first of all',
  'for instance',
  'as a result'.
- There is paragraphing to mark the main sections.
- There is a suitable conclusion to round off the writing.

Spelling Test Answers

Note to the Parent
Follow the instructions to administer and mark your child's spelling test.

Instructions for administering the Spelling Test

1) Detach this page **along the dotted line.**
It contains:
* instructions on how to administer the test
* the passage that you will read out during the test (page 19) and,
* the answers to the test.

2) Tell your child what you intend to do. Instruct him or her to read their own set of instructions as well (page 18).

3) Before you read out the passage, read the following '**Tips for Writing the Spelling Test**', out loud to your child:
* **As you write**, **say the words slowly** in your mind, to help you with their **shape.**
* If you don't know the word that is read out, try thinking of another that **sounds similar**. This is called forming a word pattern and can help you to spell the word correctly.
* When you have finished the spelling test, **look back at each word** and say it to yourself. Does it **look** right?
* Try **breaking** the word down into '**sound-bites**', to check the spelling, e.g.
   al-ways
   admire-d
   par-tic-u-lar
   lone-ly.

4) Now read the passage, **The Dragon,** out loud to your child twice.
* Read it through once without stopping.
* Read it again more slowly. Pause at the appropriate moment, to allow your child to write the words in the spaces provided. Allow sufficient time for each of the missing words to be written in.

Checklist of spelling test words as they appear in the passage

always	crawled
admired	beautiful
particular	pieces
lonely	fullest
moved	huge
slept	could
silence	finally
suddenly	crash
intruder	coughed
appeared	plotting

45

Spelling Test Answers

Reading Passage for the Spelling Test

The Dragon

On a distant mountain there was a dark, murky cave. In this cave there was a sad, old dragon.

The dragon was sad because he was <u>always</u> alone. Every day he <u>admired</u> his treasure, but that was not enough. On this <u>particular</u> day the dragon seemed more unbearably <u>lonely</u> than ever. It was winter; it had snowed. Nothing outside <u>moved</u>. The world <u>slept</u> and the cavern was plunged into deep <u>silence</u>. <u>Suddenly</u>, he caught a muffled sound. Footsteps approached. Was it an <u>intruder</u>? A figure <u>appeared</u>. It was Sven the Viking, hunting for treasure. He <u>crawled</u> into the entrance, not noticing the dragon.

Soon he was fascinated by the <u>beautiful</u> objects before him. Right at the top of the hoard, lay the finest <u>pieces</u> of all, but they were out of reach. He climbed up some way and then stretched out his arm to its <u>fullest</u> extent, but as he reached out, the <u>huge</u> pile gave way. He was so surprised that he <u>could</u> not keep his balance and fell with it, <u>finally</u> landing on the floor with a loud <u>crash</u>, a cascade of gold tumbling to his feet. By now, the dragon had seen enough, so he <u>coughed</u> loudly to warn of his presence. The terrified Sven was then dismayed to see the creature's massive length advancing towards him. Had he been hiding in the corner <u>plotting</u> to kill the Viking?

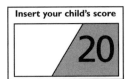

Handwriting Test Answers

Assess your handwriting

Note to the Parent
Compare your child's copy of the handwriting passage with these examples.
Decide which best matches his or her achievements.

The handwriting is legible but uneven.
1 mark

This example shows better control. Letters and spacing are beginning to look more even.
2 marks

The letters here are correctly formed. Letters and words are well spaced, printed or partially joined.
3 marks

These letters are joined confidently. They are neat and clear.
4 marks

An attractive style. This is neat and controlled.
5 marks

Insert your child's score

5

Finding your child's level

Note to the Parent

Follow the instructions to work out the approximate level your child has obtained. The **total possible number of marks** for the different sections of the test **are:**

Test	Total mark
Reading (Story A)	38
Reading (Information B,C)	12
Writing	30
Spelling	10
Handwriting	5
GRAND TOTAL	**95**

1) First **enter all the writing test marks** to get the total Writing score:

Purpose and Organisation	
Grammar	
Style	
TOTAL	

2) Now **convert the spelling mark**:

No. of words correctly spelt	Spelling test mark
1 - 2	1
3 - 4	2
5 - 6	3
7 - 8	4
9 - 10	5
11 - 12	6
13 - 14	7
15 - 16	8
17 - 18	9
19 - 20	10

3) Then, **insert each** individual **mark** scored, **onto the chart** below. Note, the reading test mark requires no conversion:

Test	Mark scored
Reading (story)	
Reading (information)	
Writing	
Spelling	
Handwriting	